# ALIVE AND NOT ALIVE

### by Gini Holland

**Reading consultant:** Susan Nations, M.Ed., author/literacy coach/
consultant in literacy development

## WEEKLY READER®
### PUBLISHING

**Please visit our web site at: www.garethstevens.com**
**For a free color catalog describing our list of high-quality books,**
**call 1-800-542-2595 (USA) or 1-800-387-3178 (Canada).**
**Our fax: 1-877-547-2596**

**Library of Congress Cataloging-in-Publication Data**

Holland, Gini.
    Alive and not alive / Gini Holland.
      p. cm. — (I know opposites)
      ISBN: 978-0-8368-8293-3 (lib. bdg.)
      ISBN: 978-0-8368-8298-8 (softcover)
      1. Life (Biology)—Juvenile literature. I. Title.
    QH501.H63   2008
    570—dc22                 2007006686

This edition first published in 2008 by
**Weekly Reader® Books**
An imprint of Gareth Stevens Publishing
1 Reader's Digest Road
Pleasantville, NY 10570-7000 USA

Copyright © 2008 by Gareth Stevens, Inc.

Managing editor: Valerie J. Weber
Art direction: Tammy West
Graphic designer: David Kowalski
Photo researcher: Diane Laska-Swanke
Production: Jessica Yanke

Picture credits: Cover (left), title page (left), pp. 8, 13, 16 (upper right) © Tony
Freeman/PhotoEdit; cover (right), title page (right), pp. 5, 6, 7, 9, 14, 15, 16 (upper left
and lower left) © Diane Laska-Swanke; p. 4 © George D. Lepp/CORBIS; pp. 10, 16
(lower right) © Craig Tuttle/CORBIS; p. 11 © Robert Brenner/PhotoEdit; p. 12 © Corel

Printed in the United States of America

2 3 4 5 6 7 8 9 11 10 09 08

# Note to Educators and Parents

Reading is such an exciting adventure for young children! They are beginning to integrate their oral language skills with written language. To encourage children along the path to early literacy, books must be colorful, engaging, and interesting; they should invite the young reader to explore both the print and the pictures.

*I Know Opposites* is a series designed to help children read and learn about the key concept of opposites. In this series, young readers learn what makes things opposite each other by exploring familiar, fun examples of things that are *Alive and Not Alive, Soft and Hard, Light and Heavy,* and *Hot and Cold.*

Each book is specially designed to support the young reader in the reading process. The familiar topics are appealing to young children and invite them to read — and re-read — again and again. The full-color photographs and enhanced text further support the student during the reading process.

In addition to serving as wonderful picture books in schools, libraries, homes, and other places where children learn to love reading, these books are specifically intended to be read within an instructional guided reading group. This small group setting allows beginning readers to work with a fluent adult model as they make meaning from the text. After children develop fluency with the text and content, the book can be read independently. Children and adults alike will find these books supportive, engaging, and fun!

— Susan Nations, M.Ed., author, literacy coach, and consultant in literacy development

The bear is alive.

# The toy bear
# is not alive.

The flower is alive.

The rock is
not alive.

# The boy is alive.

The action figure
is not alive.

# The ladybug
# is alive.

The plane is
not alive.

# The fish is alive.

The kite is not alive.

The dog is alive.

The toy dog is
not alive.

# Which are alive?

## Which are not alive?